ANIMAL MASTER

T0008938

Inky's Great Escape!

Supersmart Octopus

BY SARAH EASON
ILLUSTRATED BY LUDOVIC SALLÉ

BEARPORT
PUBLISHING

Minneapolis, Minnesota

BEAR CLAW

Credits: 20, © NaturePhoto/Shutterstock; 21, © Vladimir Wrangel/Shutterstock;
22, © Ennar0/Shutterstock; 23, © Kondratuk Aleksei/Shutterstock.

Bearport Publishing Company Product Development Team
President: Jen Jenson; Director of Product Development: Spencer Brinker;
Senior Editor: Allison Juda; Editor: Charly Haley; Associate Editor: Naomi Reich;
Senior Designer: Colin O'Dea; Associate Designer: Elena Klinkner; Associate
Designer: Kayla Eggert; Product Development Assistant: Anita Stasson

Produced by Calcium
Editor: Jennifer Sanderson; Proofreader: Harriet McGregor; Designer: Paul
Myerscough; Picture Researcher: Rachel Blount

DISCLAIMER: This graphic story is a dramatization based on true events. It is
intended to give the reader a sense of the narrative rather than a presentation
of actual details as they occurred.

Library of Congress Cataloging-in-Publication Data

Names: Eason, Sarah, author. | Salle, Ludovic, 1985- illustrator.
Title: Inky's great escape! : supersmart octopus / by Sarah Eason ;
illustrated by Ludovic Salle.
Description: Bear claw books. | Minneapolis, Minnesota : Bearport
Publishing Company, [2023] | Series: Animal masterminds | Includes
bibliographical references and index.
Identifiers: LCCN 2022033456 (print) | LCCN 2022033457 (ebook) | ISBN
9798885094313 (library binding) | ISBN 9798885095532 (paperback) | ISBN
9798885096683 (ebook)
Subjects: LCSH: Octopuses--Juvenile literature. | Octopuses--Comic books,
strips, etc. | Animal intelligence--Juvenile literature. | Animal
intelligence--Comic books, strips, etc. | Wildlife rescue--Juvenile
literature. | Wildlife rescue--Comic books, strips, etc. | LCGFT:
Graphic novels.
Classification: LCC QL430.3.O2 E27 2023 (print) | LCC QL430.3.O2 (ebook)
| DDC 594/.5615--dc23/eng/20220830
LC record available at https://lccn.loc.gov/2022033456
LC ebook record available at https://lccn.loc.gov/2022033457

For more information, write to Bearport Publishing, 5357 Penn Avenue South, Minneapolis,
MN 55419.

Contents

CHAPTER 1

Taken from the Wild

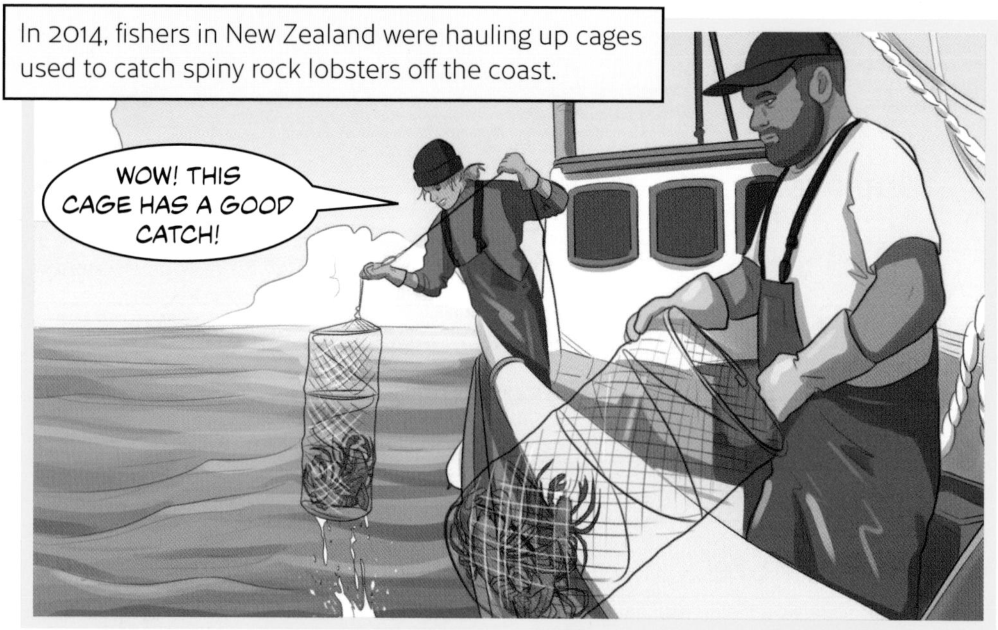
In 2014, fishers in New Zealand were hauling up cages used to catch spiny rock lobsters off the coast.
WOW! THIS CAGE HAS A GOOD CATCH!

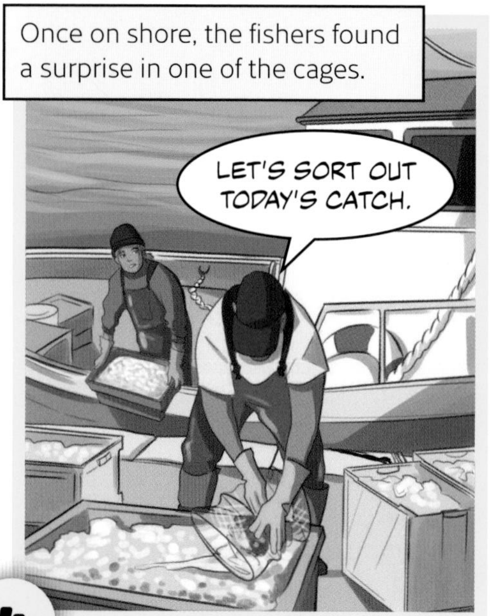
Once on shore, the fishers found a surprise in one of the cages.
LET'S SORT OUT TODAY'S CATCH.

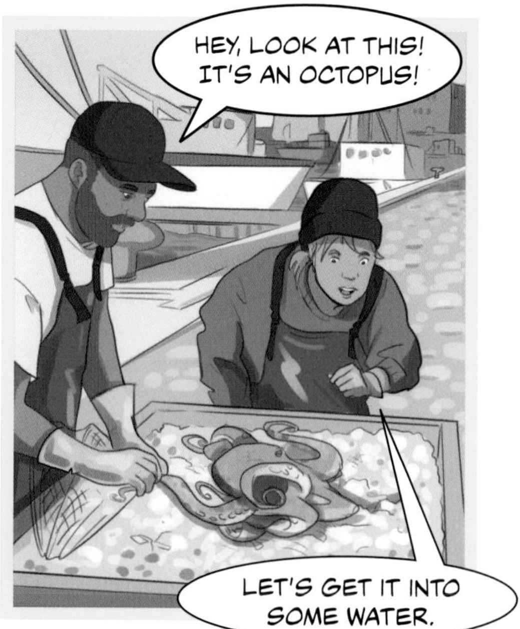
HEY, LOOK AT THIS! IT'S AN OCTOPUS!
LET'S GET IT INTO SOME WATER.

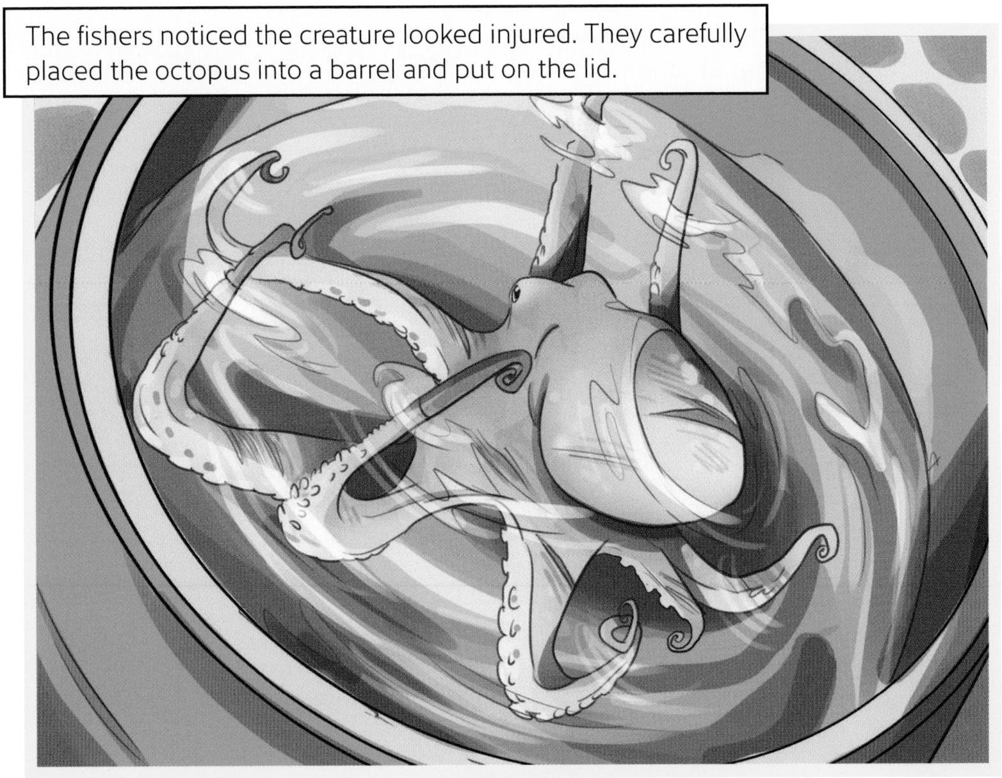
The fishers noticed the creature looked injured. They carefully placed the octopus into a barrel and put on the lid.

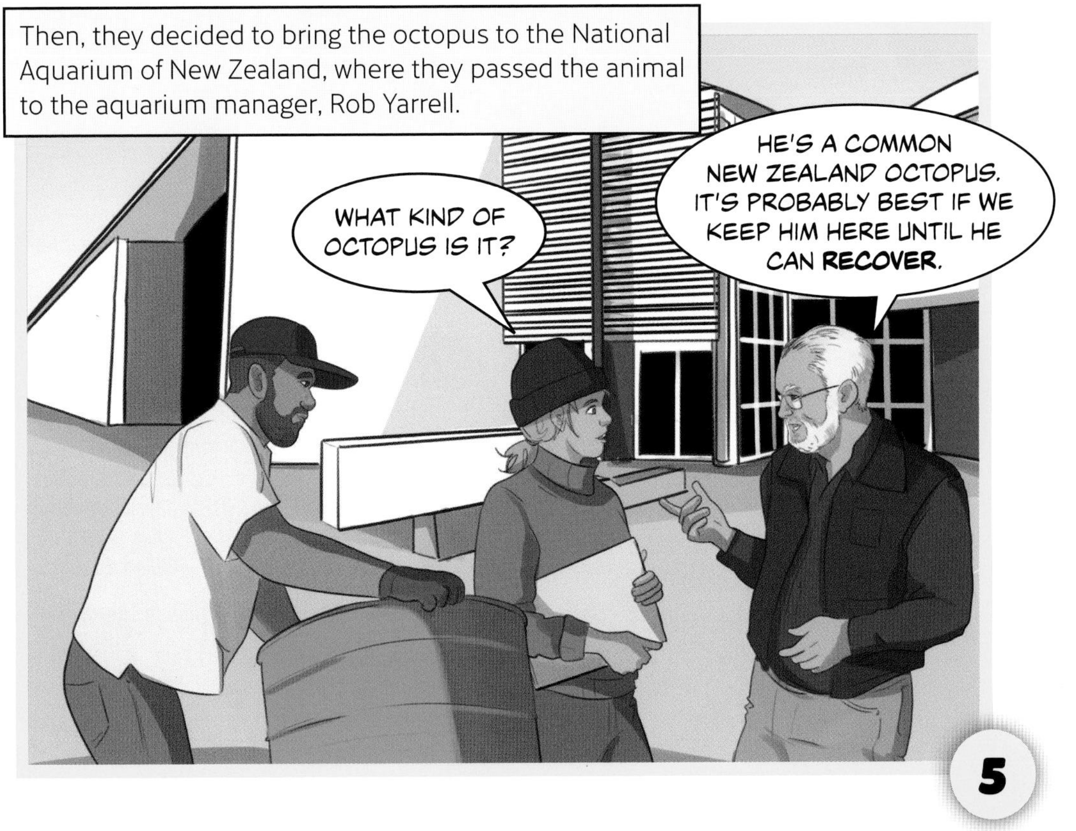
Then, they decided to bring the octopus to the National Aquarium of New Zealand, where they passed the animal to the aquarium manager, Rob Yarrell.
WHAT KIND OF OCTOPUS IS IT?
HE'S A COMMON NEW ZEALAND OCTOPUS. IT'S PROBABLY BEST IF WE KEEP HIM HERE UNTIL HE CAN **RECOVER**.

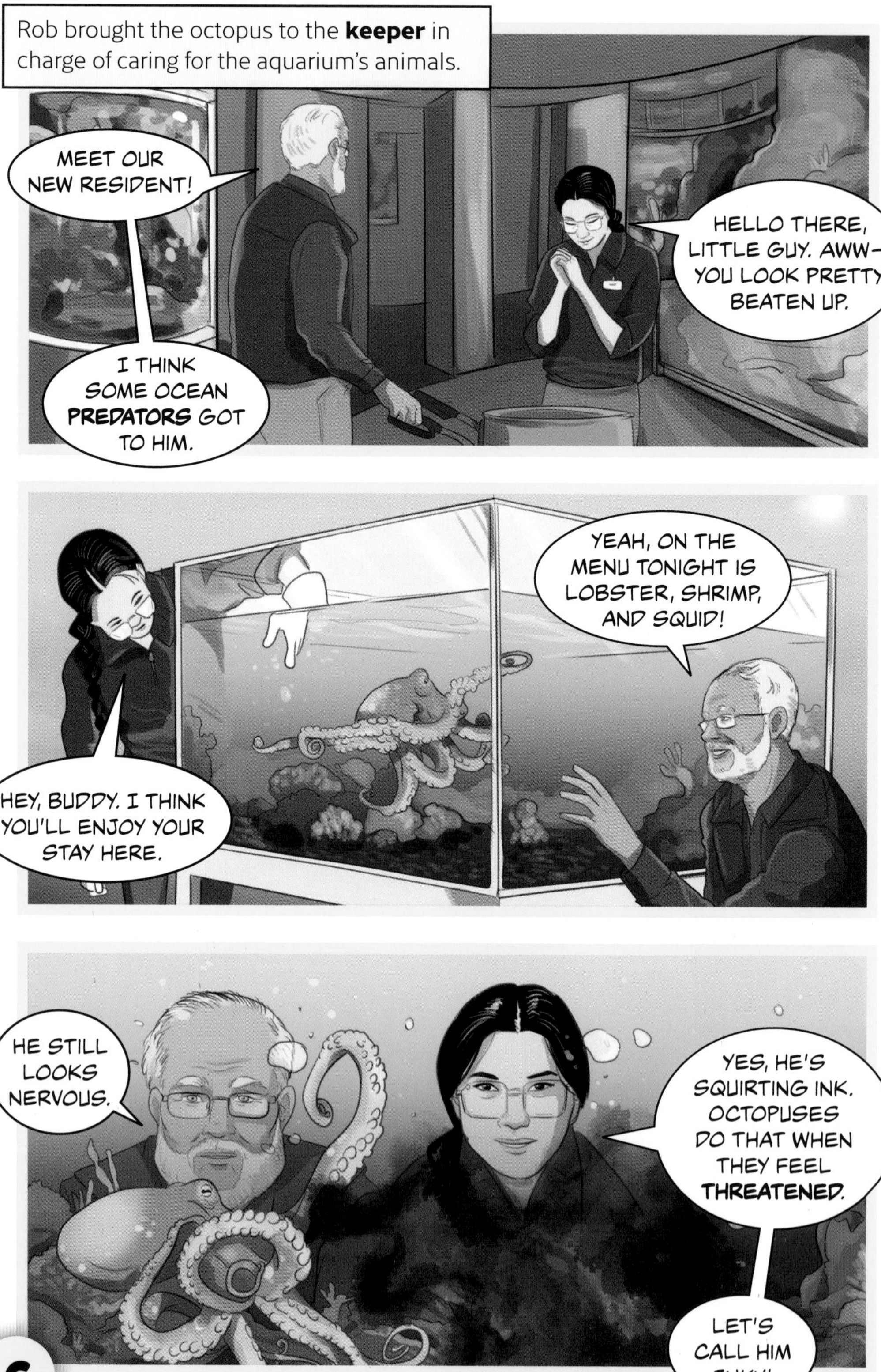
Rob brought the octopus to the **keeper** in charge of caring for the aquarium's animals.
MEET OUR NEW RESIDENT!
I THINK SOME OCEAN **PREDATORS** GOT TO HIM.
HELLO THERE, LITTLE GUY. AWW— YOU LOOK PRETTY BEATEN UP.
HEY, BUDDY. I THINK YOU'LL ENJOY YOUR STAY HERE.
YEAH, ON THE MENU TONIGHT IS LOBSTER, SHRIMP, AND SQUID!
HE STILL LOOKS NERVOUS.
YES, HE'S SQUIRTING INK. OCTOPUSES DO THAT WHEN THEY FEEL **THREATENED.**
LET'S CALL HIM INKY!

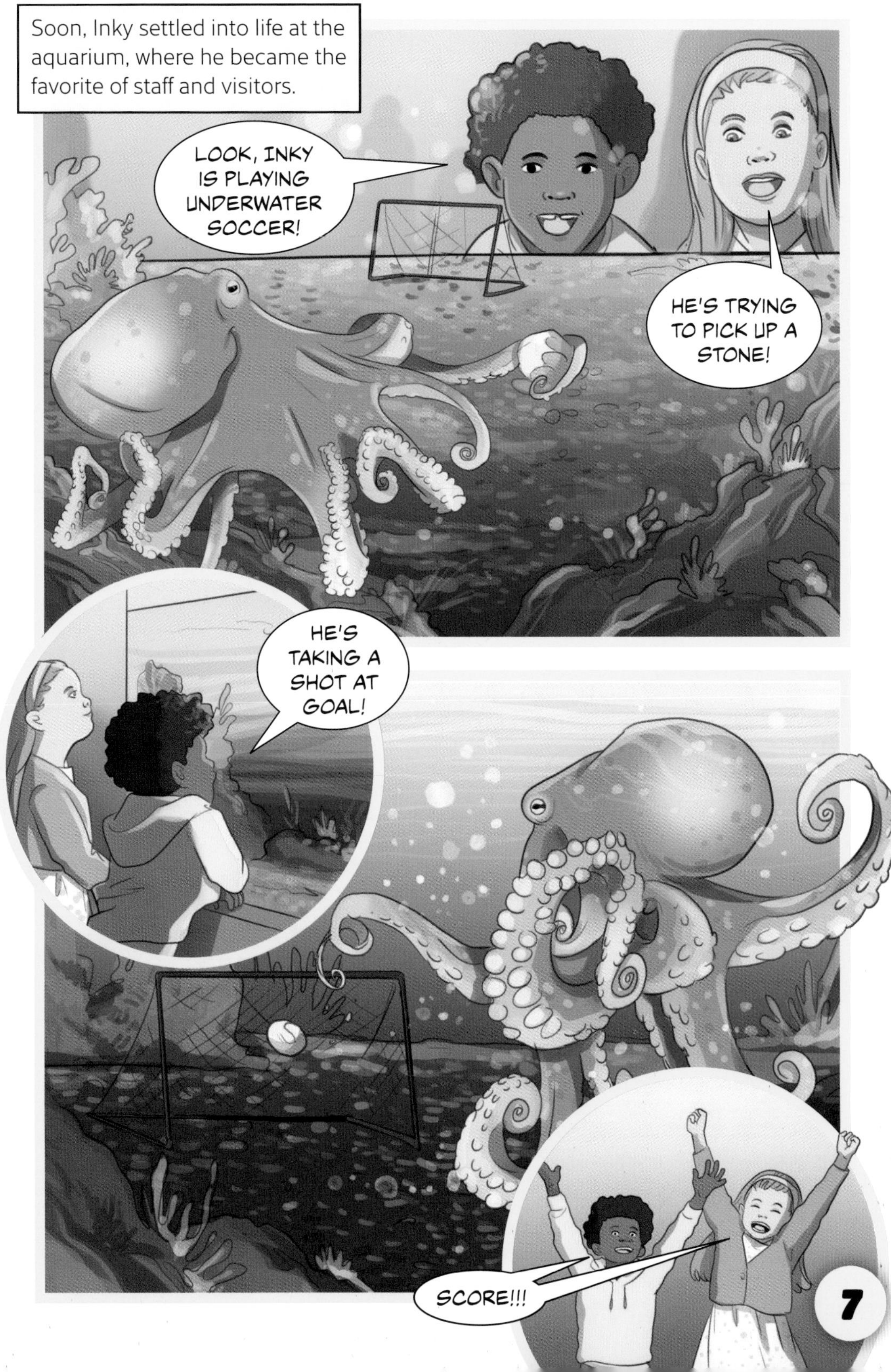
Soon, Inky settled into life at the aquarium, where he became the favorite of staff and visitors.
LOOK, INKY IS PLAYING UNDERWATER SOCCER!
HE'S TRYING TO PICK UP A STONE!
HE'S TAKING A SHOT AT GOAL!
SCORE!!!

CHAPTER 2

Smart Animals

James Wood was a **marine biologist** and octopus specialist at the aquarium.

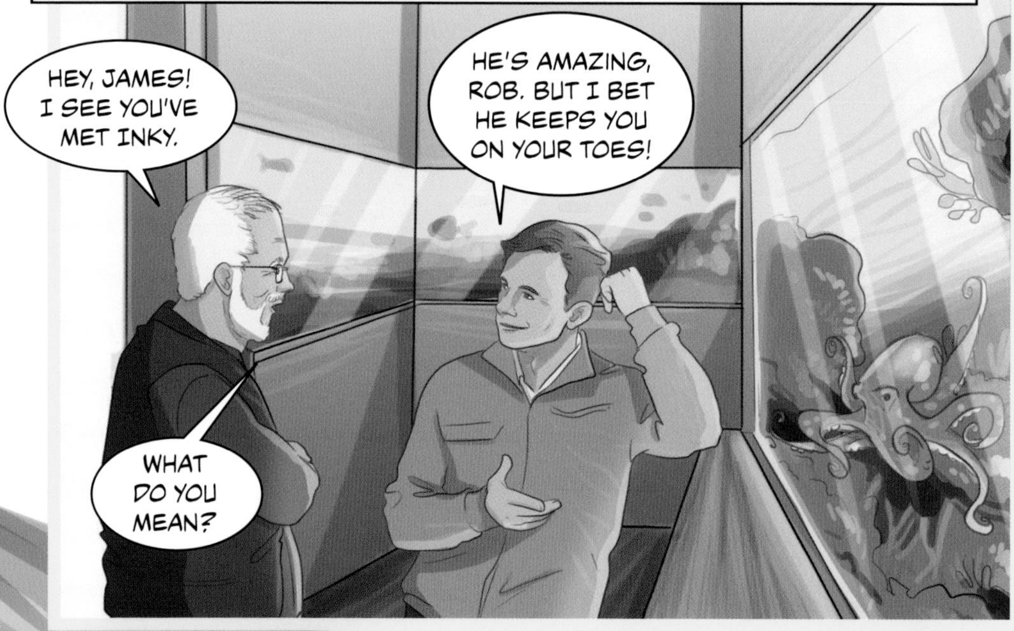
HEY, JAMES! I SEE YOU'VE MET INKY.
HE'S AMAZING, ROB. BUT I BET HE KEEPS YOU ON YOUR TOES!
WHAT DO YOU MEAN?

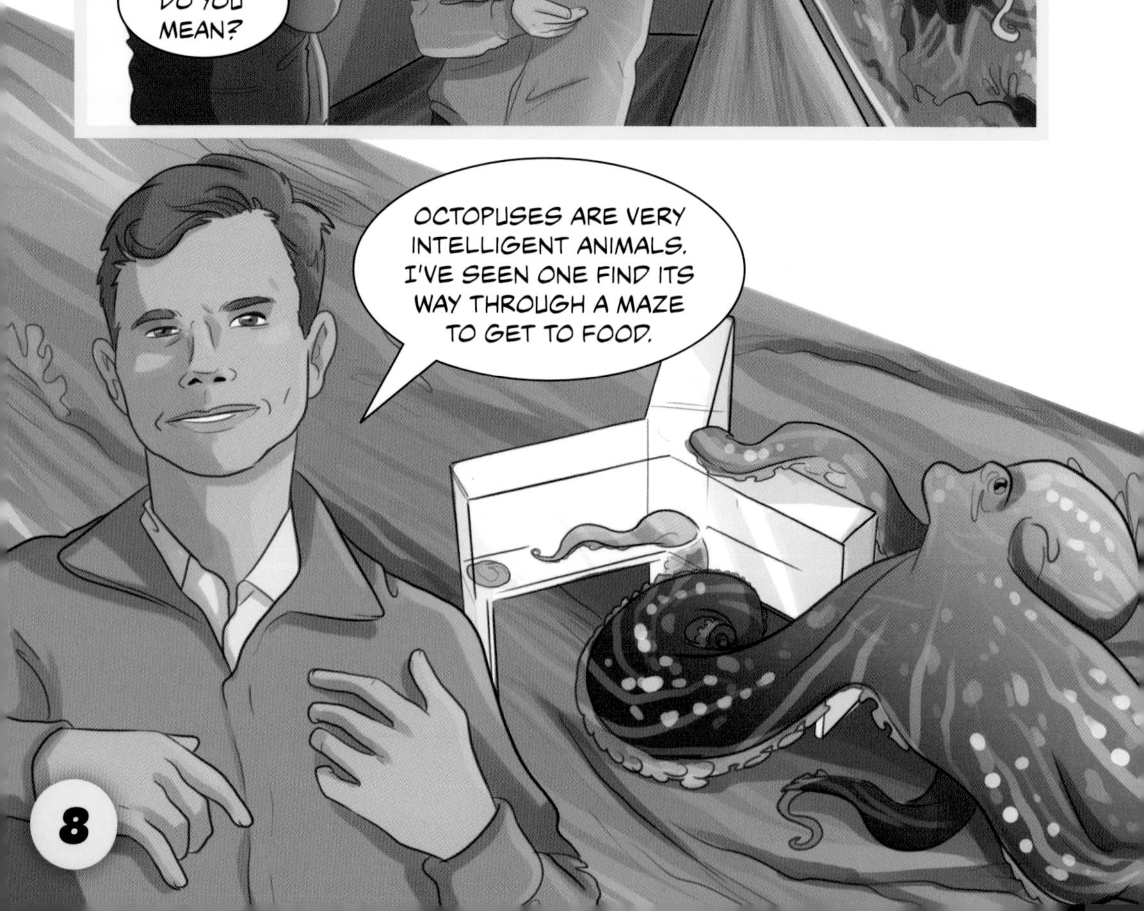
OCTOPUSES ARE VERY INTELLIGENT ANIMALS. I'VE SEEN ONE FIND ITS WAY THROUGH A MAZE TO GET TO FOOD.

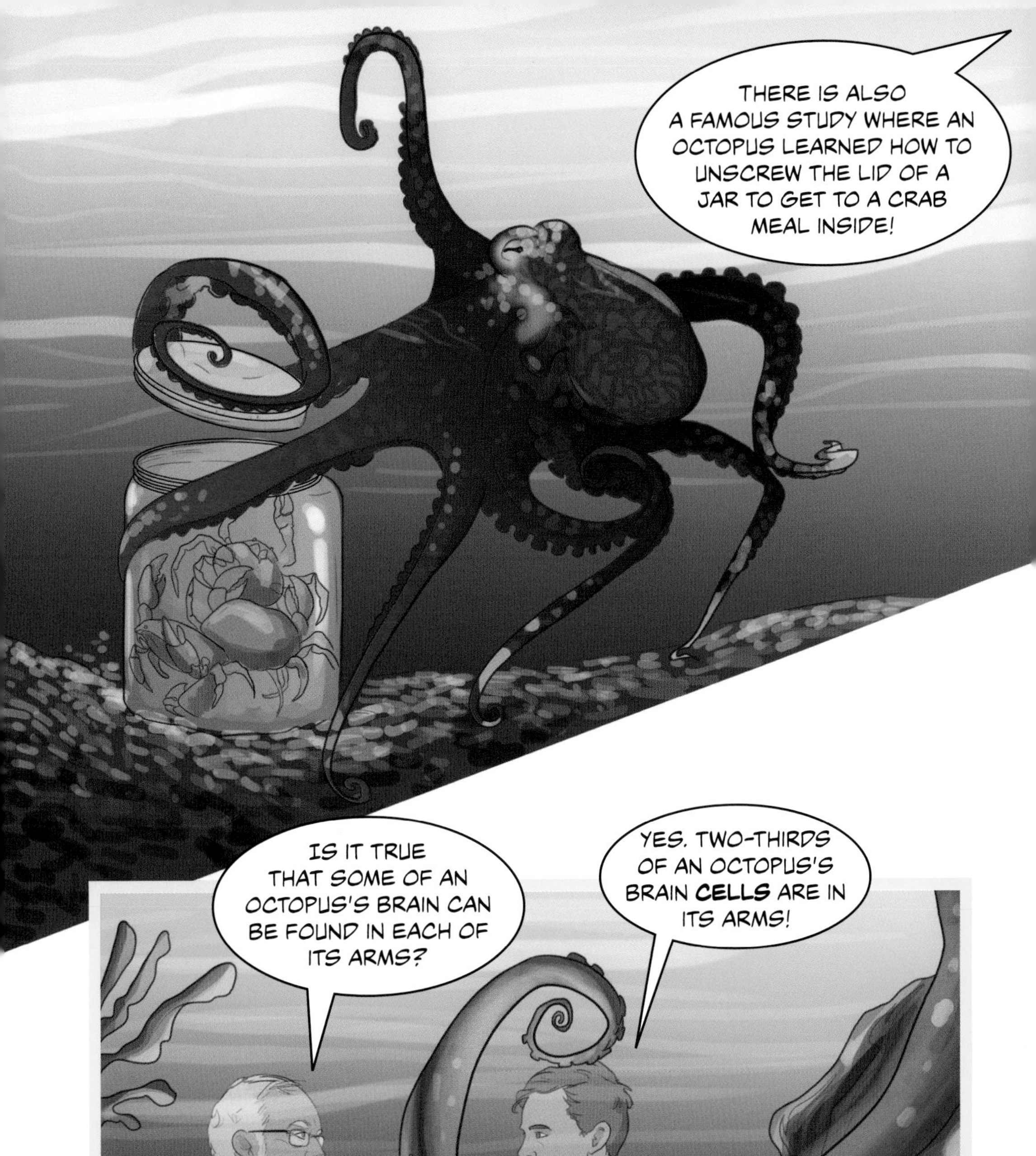
THERE IS ALSO A FAMOUS STUDY WHERE AN OCTOPUS LEARNED HOW TO UNSCREW THE LID OF A JAR TO GET TO A CRAB MEAL INSIDE!

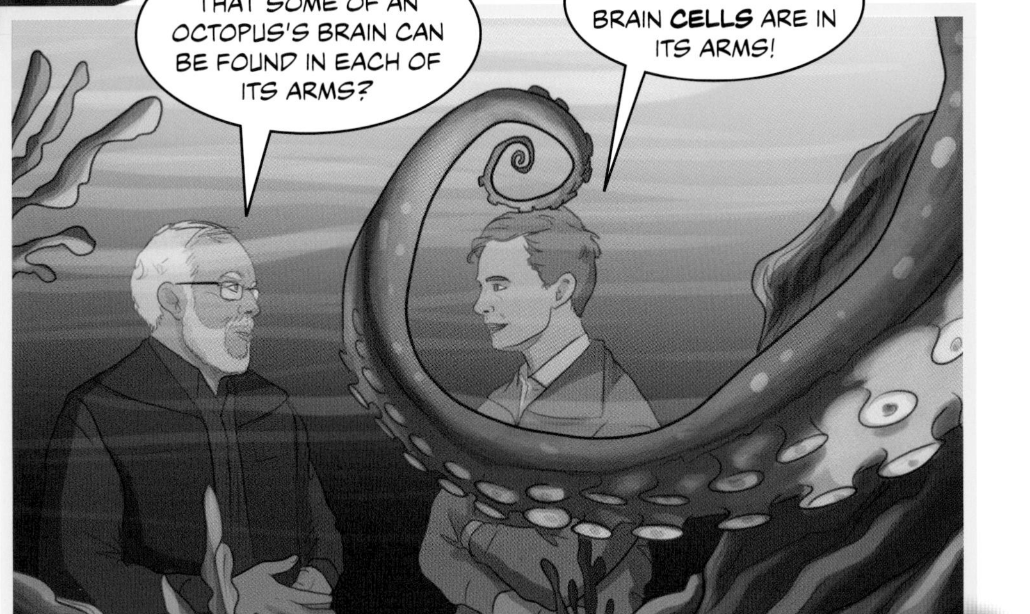
IS IT TRUE THAT SOME OF AN OCTOPUS'S BRAIN CAN BE FOUND IN EACH OF ITS ARMS?
YES. TWO-THIRDS OF AN OCTOPUS'S BRAIN **CELLS** ARE IN ITS ARMS!

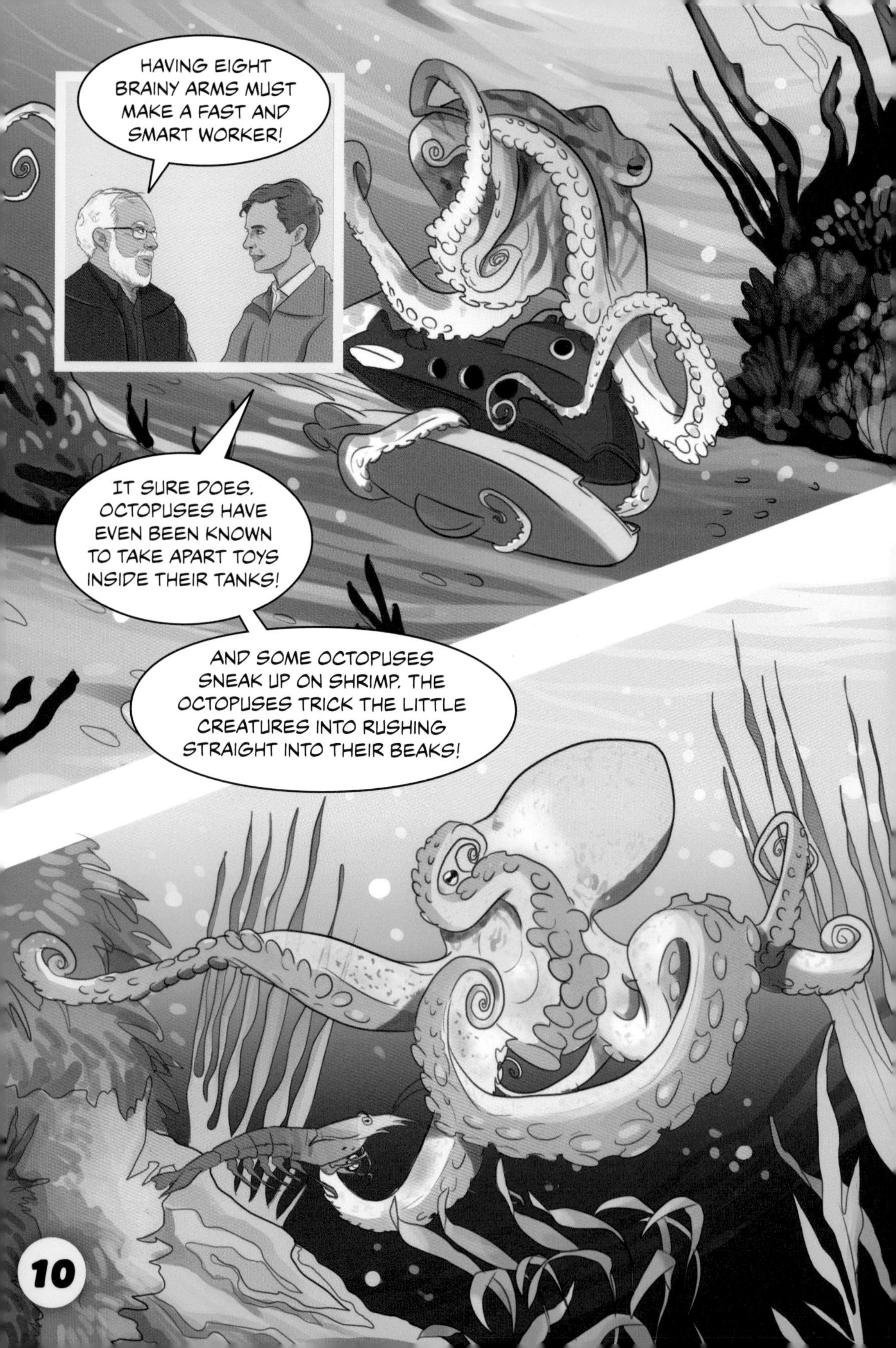
HAVING EIGHT BRAINY ARMS MUST MAKE A FAST AND SMART WORKER!
IT SURE DOES. OCTOPUSES HAVE EVEN BEEN KNOWN TO TAKE APART TOYS INSIDE THEIR TANKS!
AND SOME OCTOPUSES SNEAK UP ON SHRIMP. THE OCTOPUSES TRICK THE LITTLE CREATURES INTO RUSHING STRAIGHT INTO THEIR BEAKS!

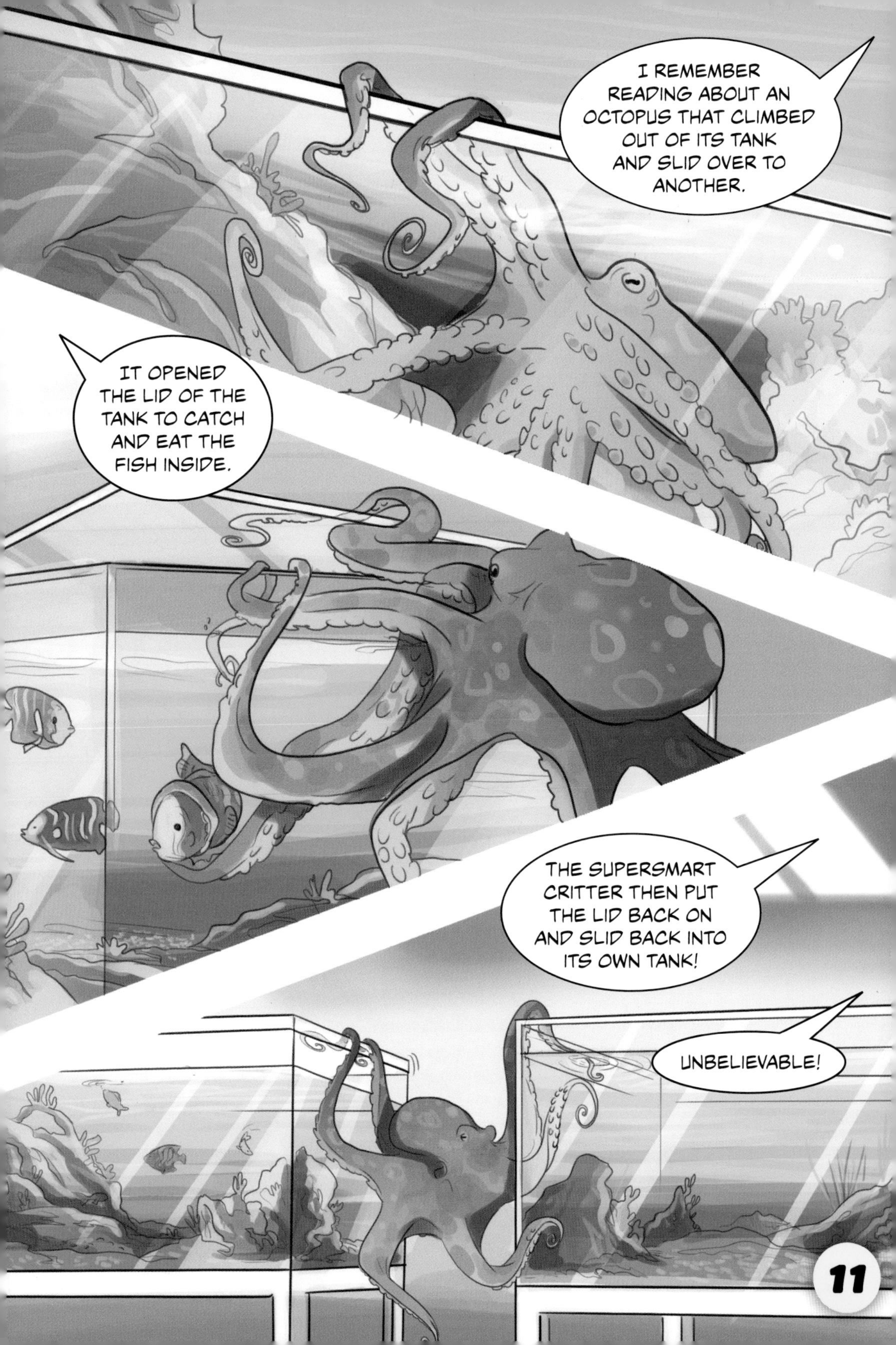
I REMEMBER READING ABOUT AN OCTOPUS THAT CLIMBED OUT OF ITS TANK AND SLID OVER TO ANOTHER.
IT OPENED THE LID OF THE TANK TO CATCH AND EAT THE FISH INSIDE.
THE SUPERSMART CRITTER THEN PUT THE LID BACK ON AND SLID BACK INTO ITS OWN TANK!
UNBELIEVABLE!

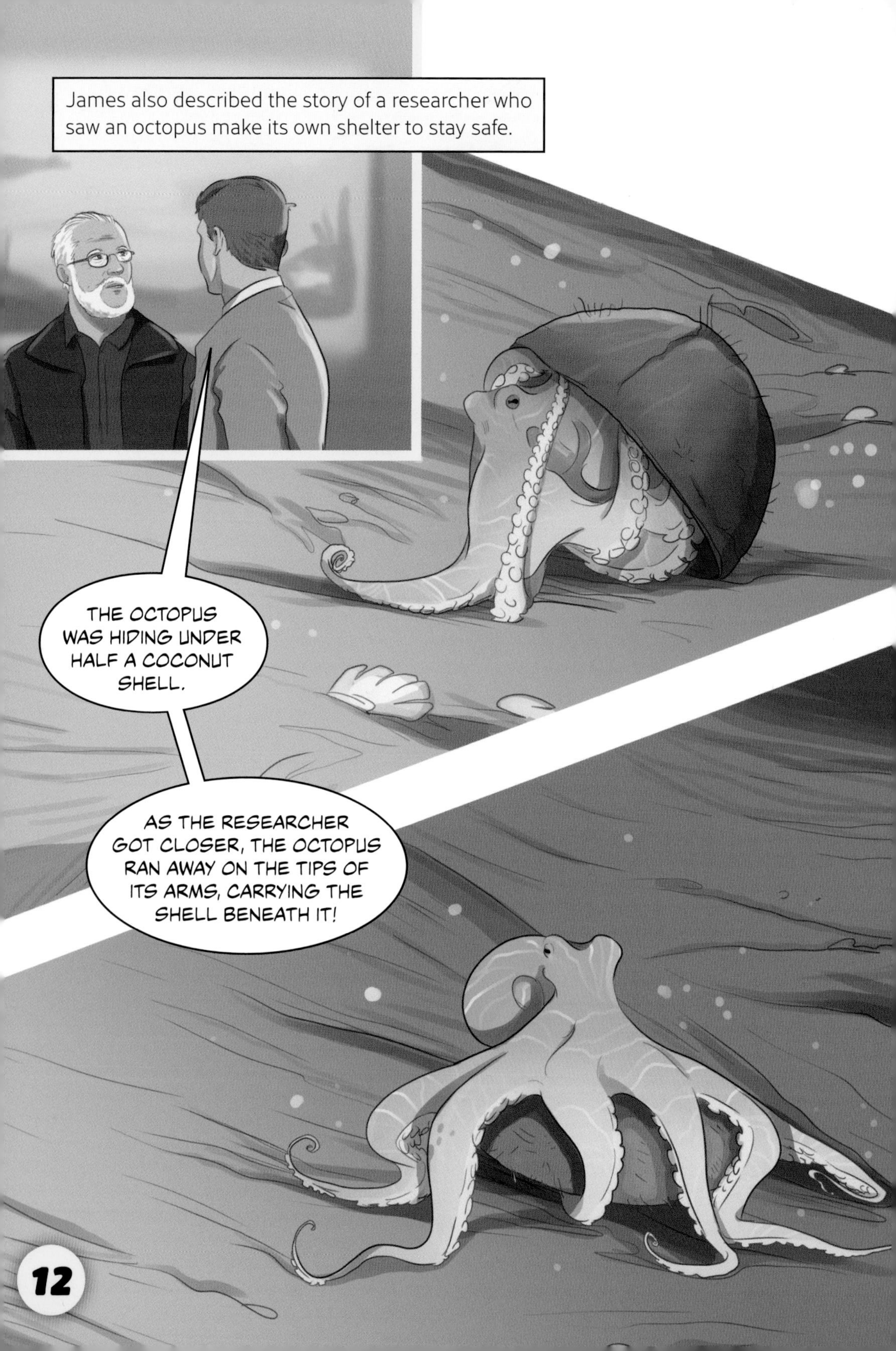
James also described the story of a researcher who saw an octopus make its own shelter to stay safe.
THE OCTOPUS WAS HIDING UNDER HALF A COCONUT SHELL.
AS THE RESEARCHER GOT CLOSER, THE OCTOPUS RAN AWAY ON THE TIPS OF ITS ARMS, CARRYING THE SHELL BENEATH IT!

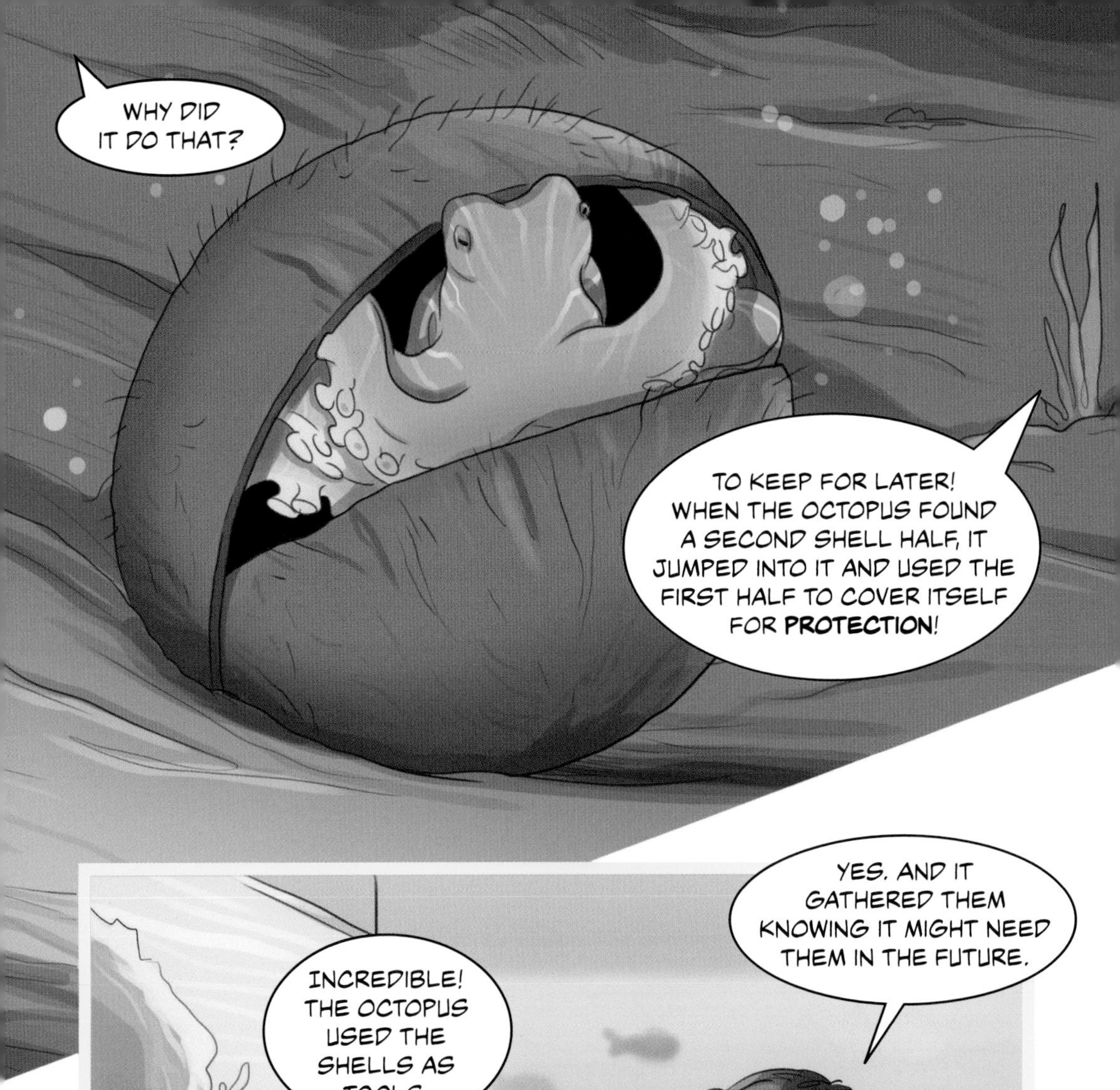
WHY DID IT DO THAT?
TO KEEP FOR LATER! WHEN THE OCTOPUS FOUND A SECOND SHELL HALF, IT JUMPED INTO IT AND USED THE FIRST HALF TO COVER ITSELF FOR **PROTECTION**!

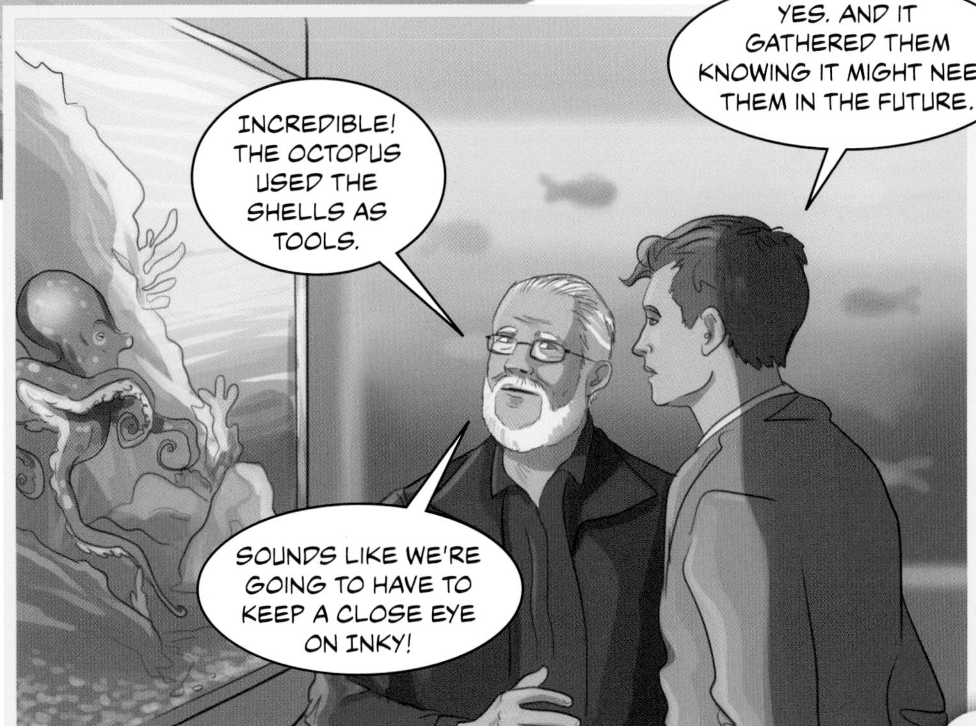
INCREDIBLE! THE OCTOPUS USED THE SHELLS AS TOOLS.
YES. AND IT GATHERED THEM KNOWING IT MIGHT NEED THEM IN THE FUTURE.
SOUNDS LIKE WE'RE GOING TO HAVE TO KEEP A CLOSE EYE ON INKY!

CHAPTER 3

Inky Makes His Escape

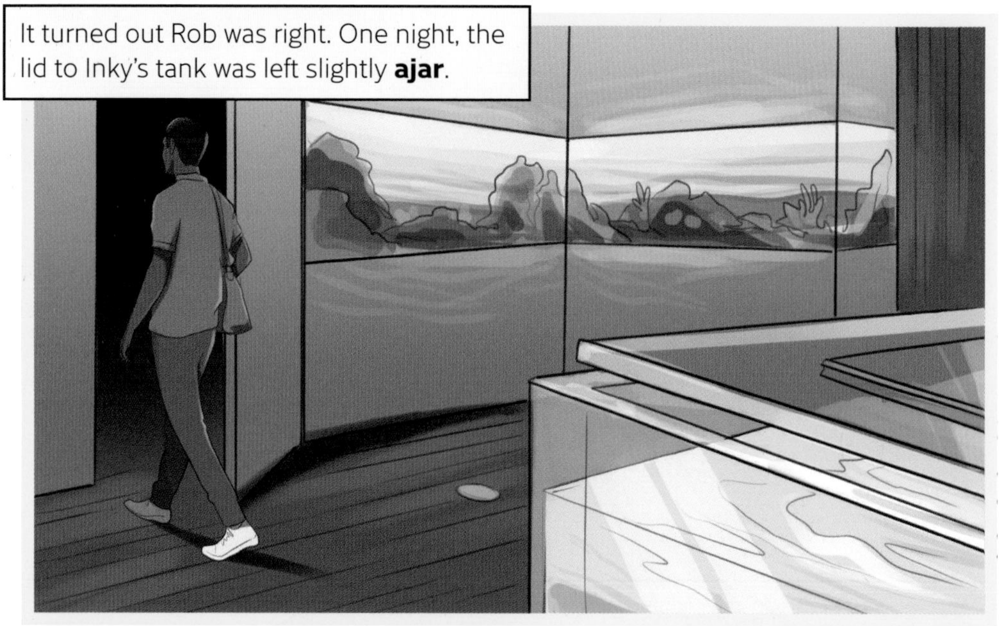
It turned out Rob was right. One night, the lid to Inky's tank was left slightly **ajar**.

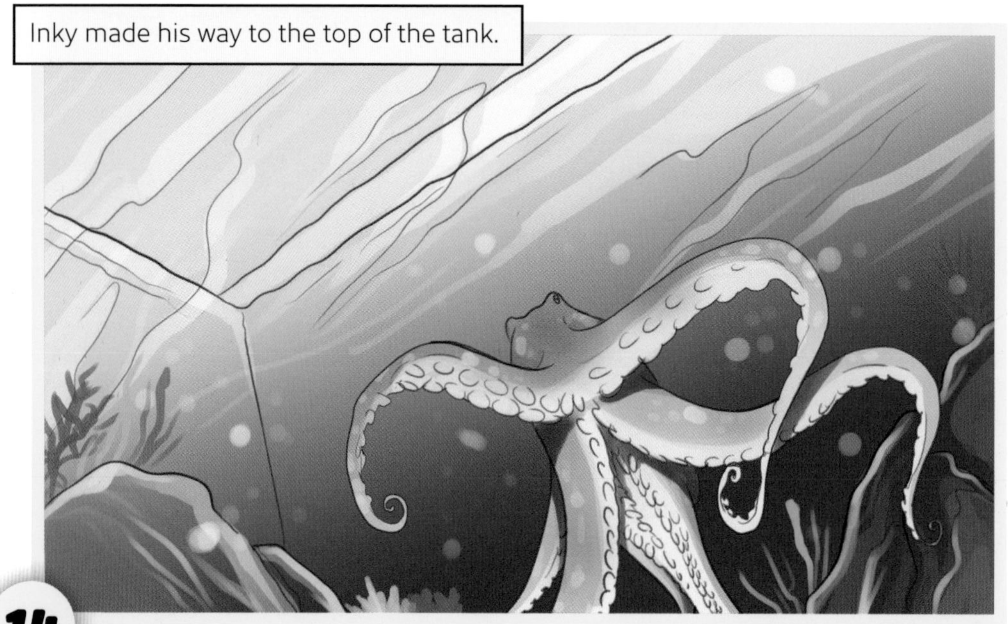
Inky made his way to the top of the tank.

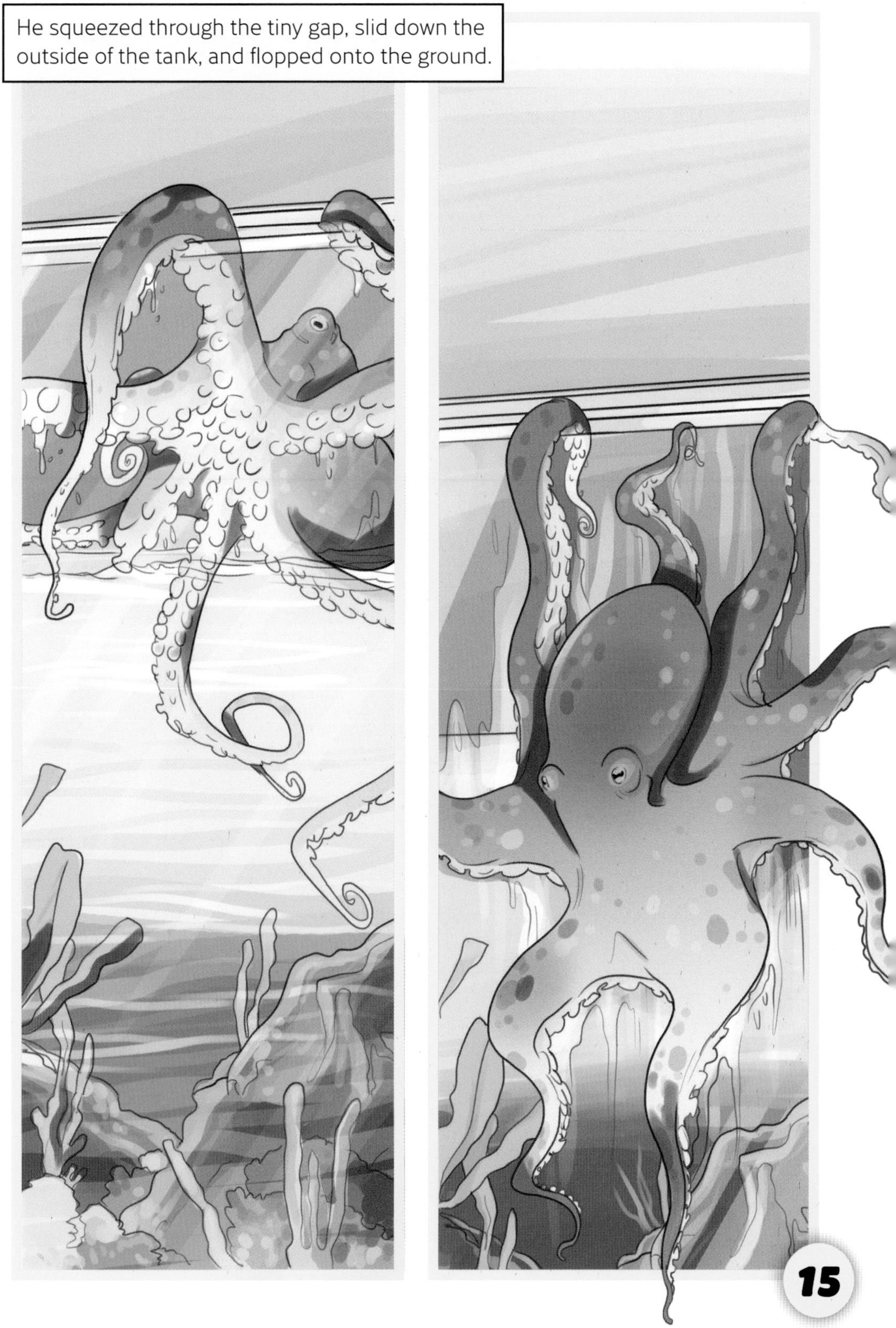
He squeezed through the tiny gap, slid down the outside of the tank, and flopped onto the ground.

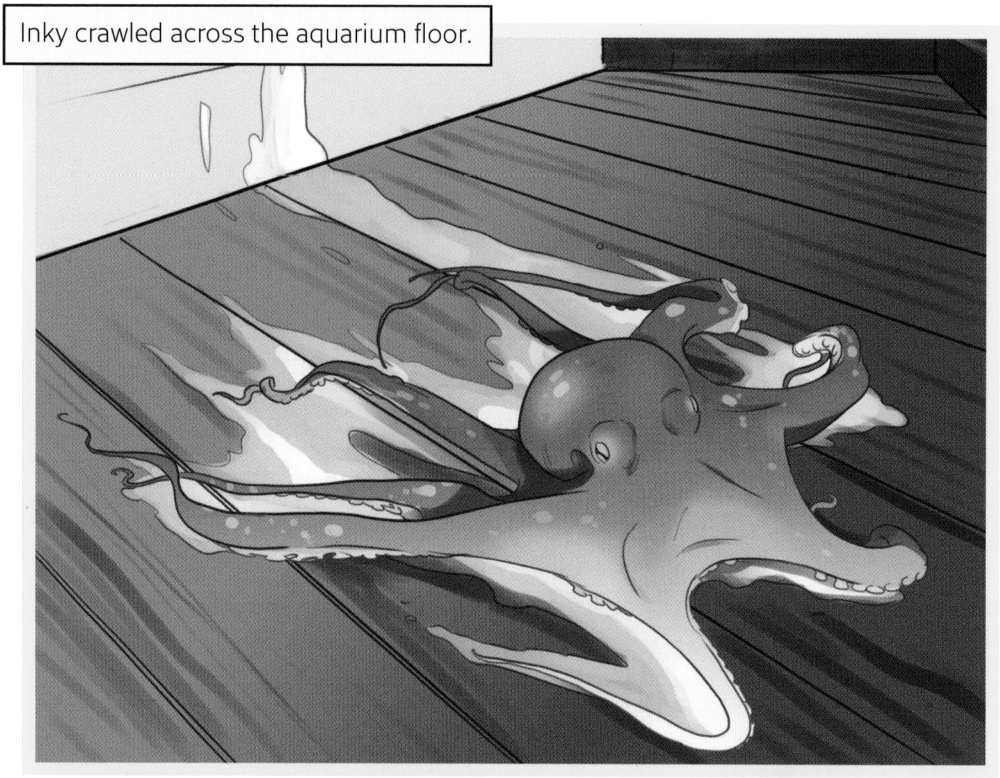
Inky crawled across the aquarium floor.

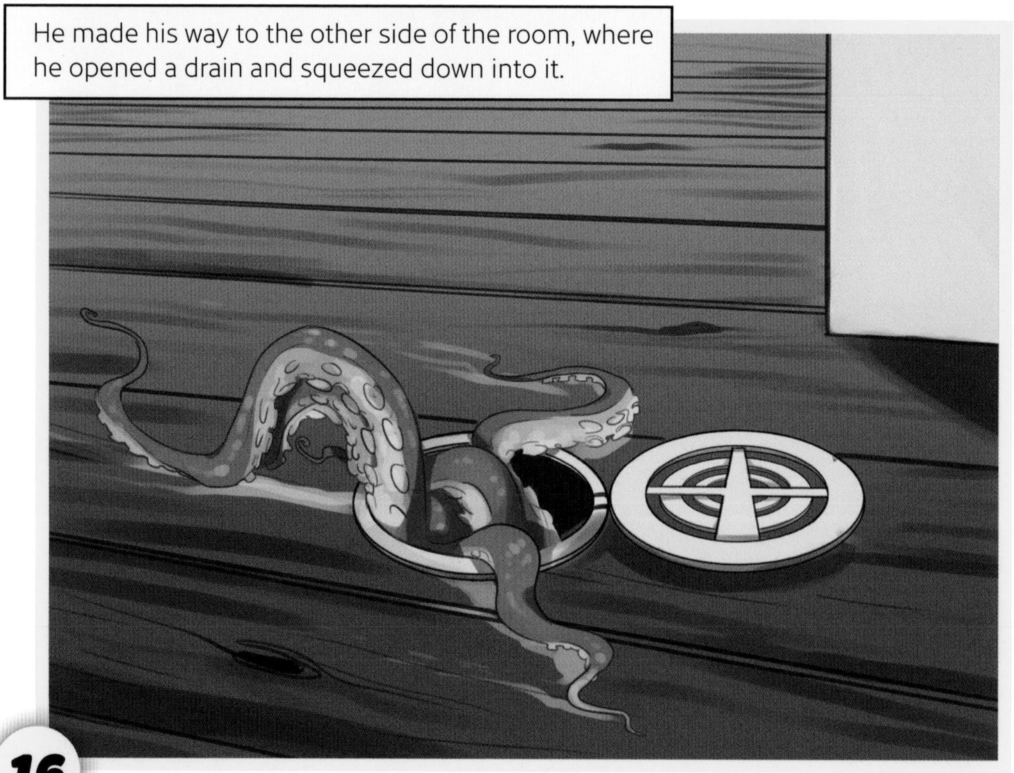
He made his way to the other side of the room, where he opened a drain and squeezed down into it.

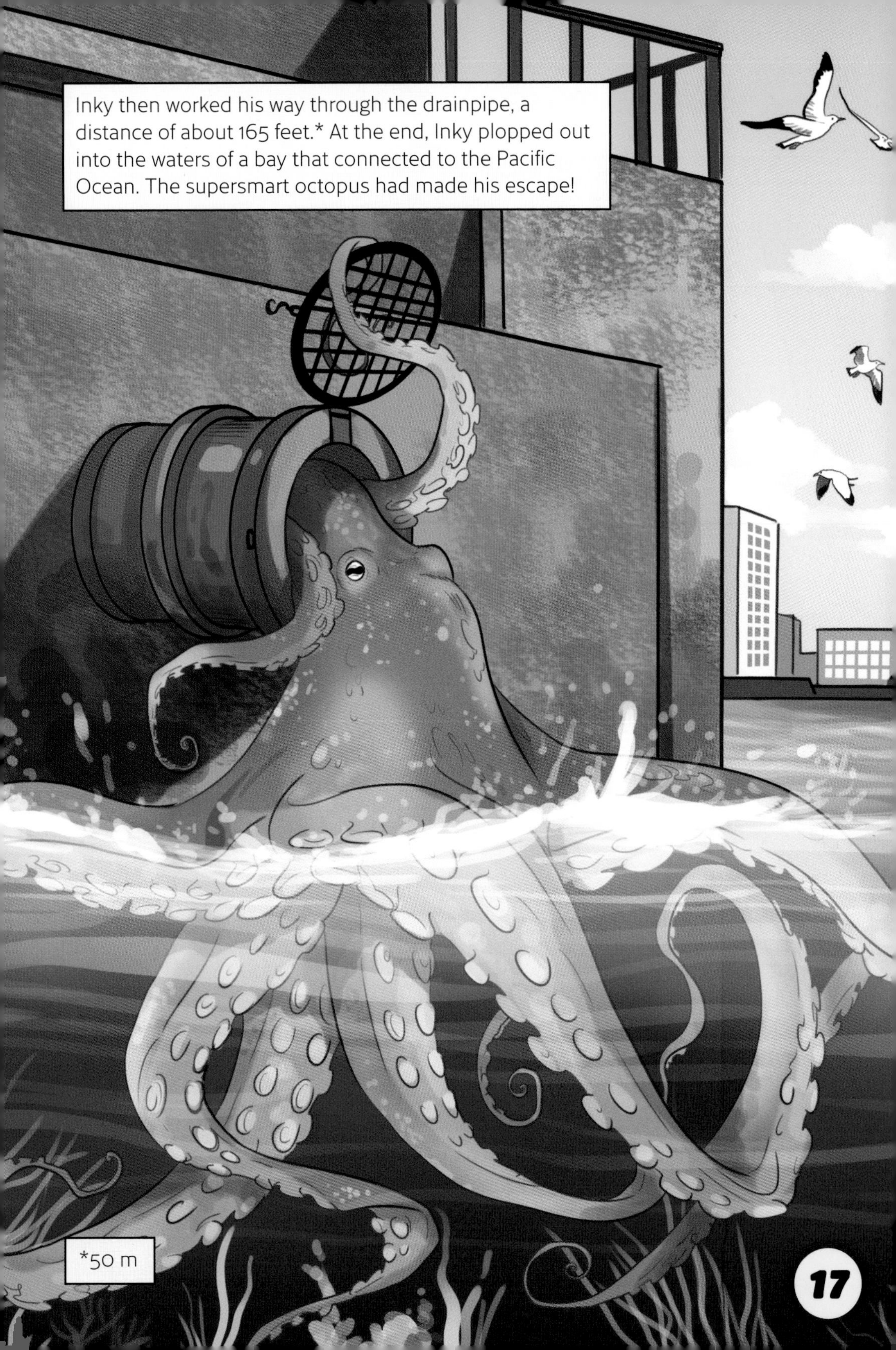
Inky then worked his way through the drainpipe, a distance of about 165 feet.* At the end, Inky plopped out into the waters of a bay that connected to the Pacific Ocean. The supersmart octopus had made his escape!
*50 m

Inky's story became headline news! Everyone wanted to know how Inky had managed to escape.

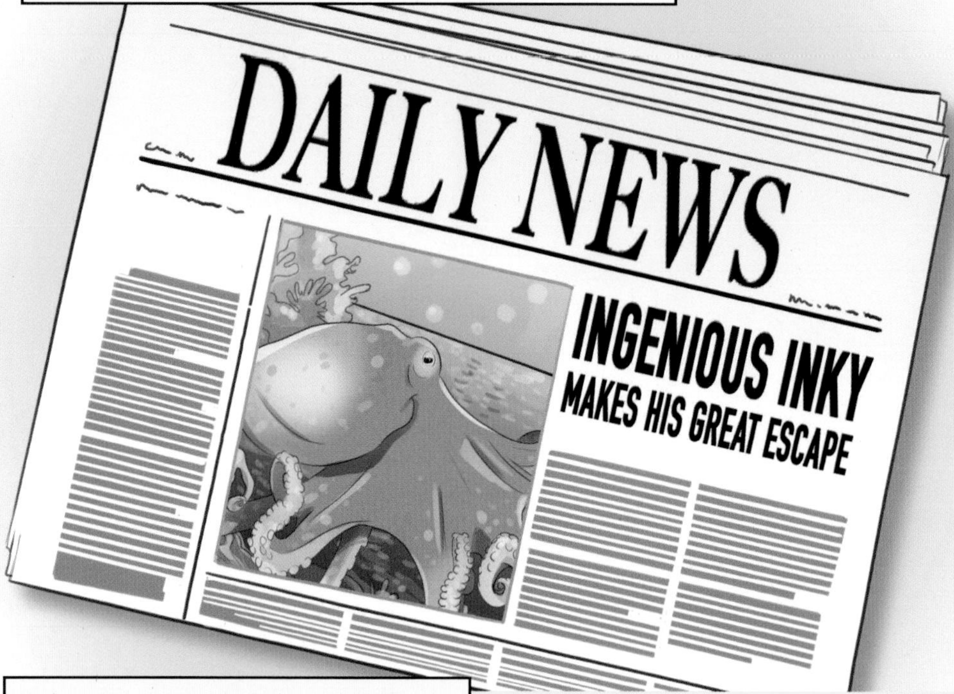
DAILY NEWS
INGENIOUS INKY
MAKES HIS GREAT ESCAPE

Rob was interviewed about Inky's tale.

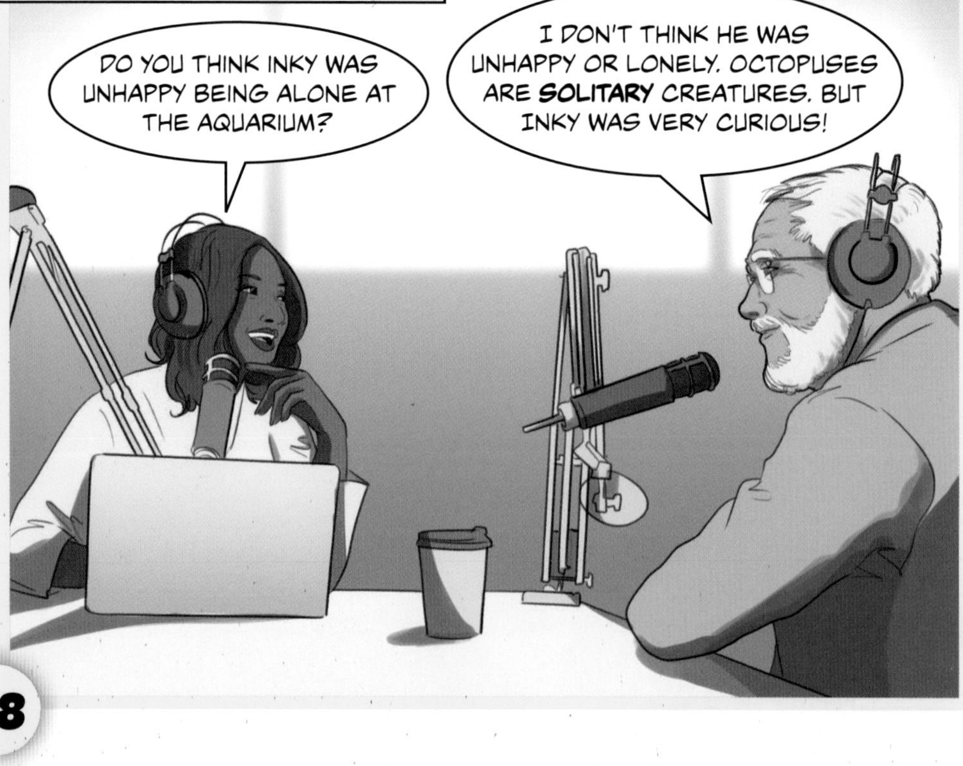
DO YOU THINK INKY WAS UNHAPPY BEING ALONE AT THE AQUARIUM?
I DON'T THINK HE WAS UNHAPPY OR LONELY. OCTOPUSES ARE **SOLITARY** CREATURES. BUT INKY WAS VERY CURIOUS!

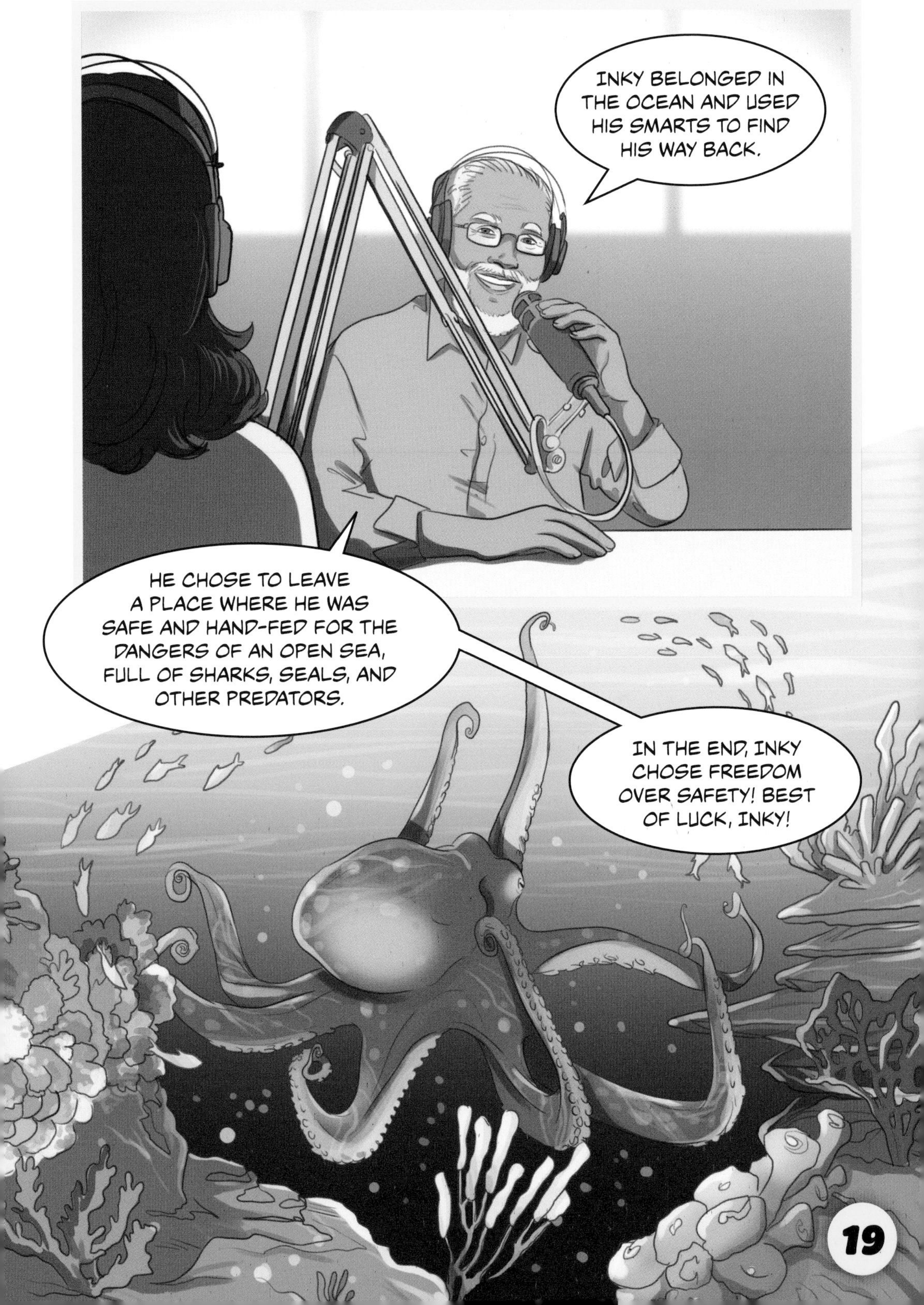
INKY BELONGED IN THE OCEAN AND USED HIS SMARTS TO FIND HIS WAY BACK.
HE CHOSE TO LEAVE A PLACE WHERE HE WAS SAFE AND HAND-FED FOR THE DANGERS OF AN OPEN SEA, FULL OF SHARKS, SEALS, AND OTHER PREDATORS.
IN THE END, INKY CHOSE FREEDOM OVER SAFETY! BEST OF LUCK, INKY!

All about Octopuses

Octopuses can squeeze their bodies into tight spaces. That is because they are **invertebrates**—animals that do not have skeletons.

- An octopus has a hard beak, similar to that of a bird. It uses its beak to break open the shells of crabs and shellfish. Then, the octopus eats the fleshy parts.

- Some octopuses **camouflage** themselves to hide from predators. For example, if an octopus is near a rocky area, it can change color to match the rocks. That helps it blend in, making it difficult for predators to see.

THIS OCTOPUS USES CAMOUFLAGE TO BLEND IN WITH ITS REEF HOME.

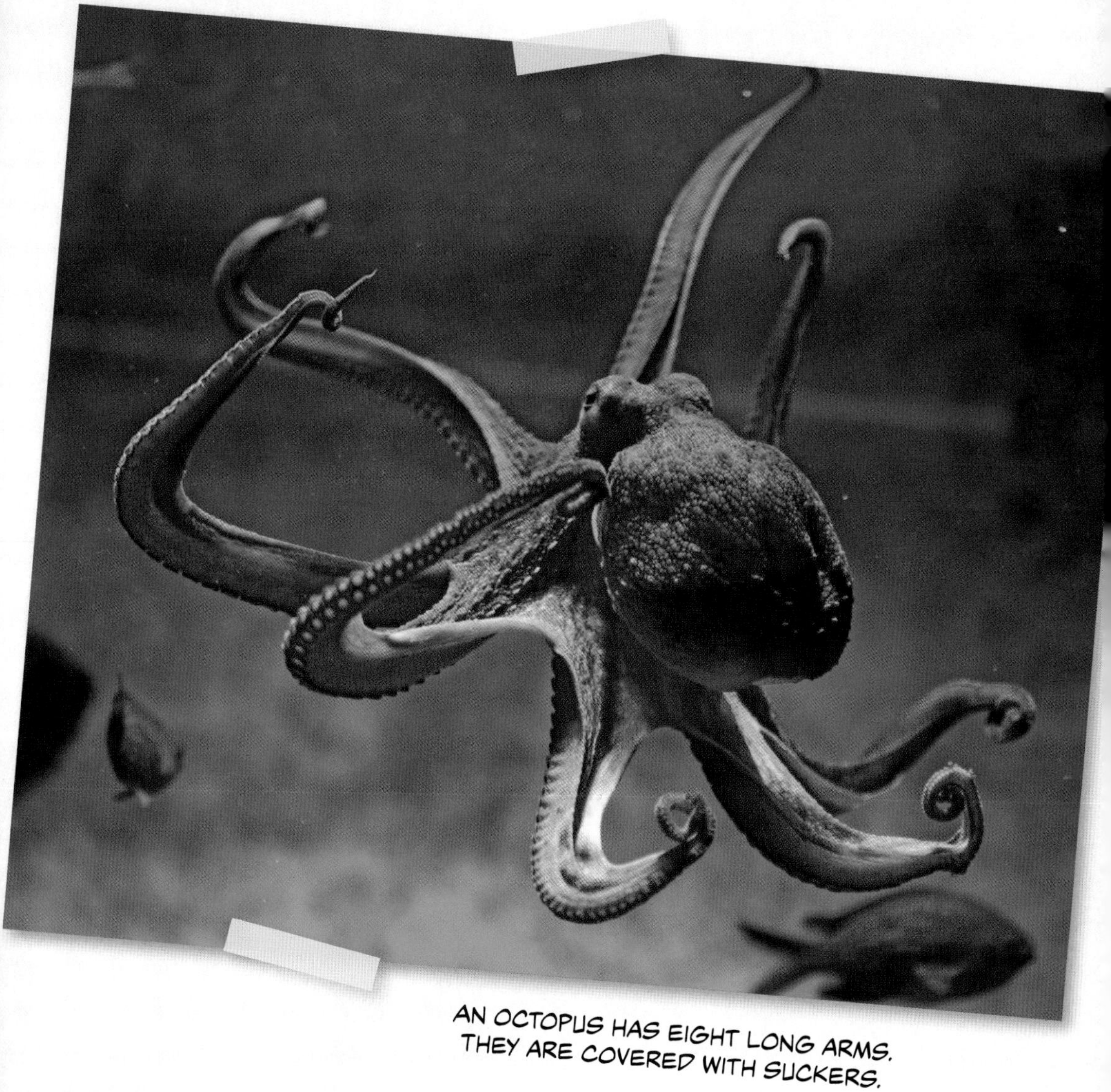

AN OCTOPUS HAS EIGHT LONG ARMS. THEY ARE COVERED WITH SUCKERS.

- Octopuses also protect themselves from predators by squirting ink! If an octopus is frightened, it squirts a large cloud of black ink into the water. That confuses any nearby predators. Then, the octopus can swim away.

More Smart Octopuses

Octopuses do not like bright lights, which might explain the behavior of one supersmart octopus at an aquarium in Germany. It kept its keepers on their toes by squirting water at an overhead light to turn it off. Every time the keepers fixed the light and turned it back on again, the octopus would squirt water to turn it off once more!

siphon

OCTOPUSES USE A TUBE CALLED A SIPHON TO SQUIRT WATER. THIS HELPS THEM SWIM OR STEER.

Have you heard of a picky eater with eight arms? One aquarium octopus didn't eat its frozen squid meal. Instead, it waited for the keeper to return. When she did, the octopus held the squid up, then moved toward an outflow pipe. All the while, it kept its eye on the keeper, as if trying to hold her attention. The octopus dumped the squid in the pipe, making its thoughts on the frozen meal clear!

Glossary

ajar slightly open

camouflage to use colors or patterns to blend in with one's surroundings

cells the smallest parts of all living things

invertebrates animals that do not have a backbone

keeper a person whose job is to care for animals

marine biologist a scientist who studies the oceans and the creatures that live in them

predators animals that hunt and eat other animals

protection something that keeps an animal safe

recover to get over a difficult experience or illness

solitary alone

threatened frightened or at risk of being harmed by something

INKY ISN'T THE ONLY OCTOPUS THAT HAS ESCAPED FROM ITS TANK. THERE ARE OTHER STORIES OF OCTOPUSES WHO HAVE MADE GREAT ESCAPES FROM AQUARIUMS AND RETURNED TO THEIR OCEAN HOMES.

Index

Read More

Gaertner, Meg. *Mimic Octopuses (Unique Animal Adaptations).*
North Mankato, MN: Capstone Press, 2020.

Jaycox, Jaclyn. *Octopuses (Animals).* North Mankato, MN: Capstone
Press, 2021.

Shaffer, Lindsay. *Octopuses (Animal of the Coral Reef).*
Minneapolis: Bellwether Media, 2020.

Learn More Online

1. Go to **www.factsurfer.com** or scan the QR code below.
2. Enter "**Inky's Great Escape**" into the search box.
3. Click on the cover of this book to see a list of websites.